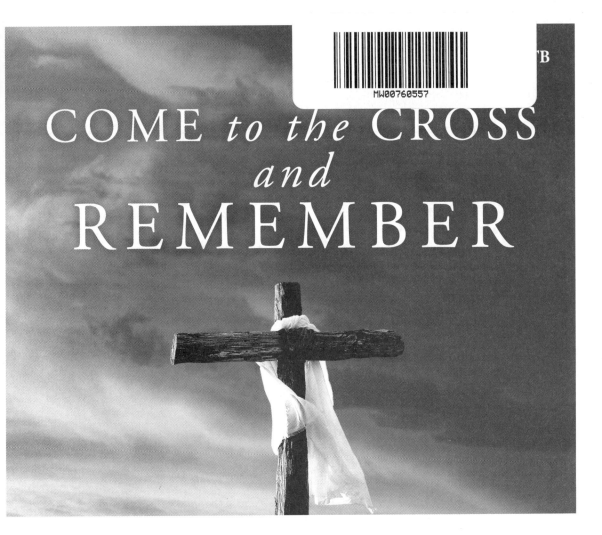

MW00760557

COME *to the* CROSS *and* REMEMBER

Pepper Choplin

Written and Arranged by Pepper Choplin
Narration by Pepper Choplin
Orchestration by Michael Lawrence

Editor: Jean Anne Shafferman
Cover Design: Katie Hufford
Music Engraving: Linda Taylor

© 2017 Lorenz Publishing Company, a division of The Lorenz Corporation. All rights reserved. Printed in the U.S.A.
Reproduction of this publication without permission of the publisher is a criminal offense subject to prosecution.

A Lorenz Company • www.lorenz.com

CONTENTS

COMPANION PRODUCTS

55/1183L	SATB Score
55/1184L	SATB Score with Performance CD
99/3664L	Bulk Performance CDs (10 pak)
99/3661L	Accompaniment CD
99/3662L	Split-track Accompaniment CD
99/3663L	SA/TB Part-dominant Rehearsal CDs, **Reproducible**

Orchestration by Michael Lawrence for 2 Fl, Ob, 2 Cl, Bsn (sub Bass Cl), 2 Hn (sub 2 A Sax), 3 Tpt, 2Tbn (sub 2 T Sax), Tuba, 2 Perc, Timp, Harp, Pno, 2 Vln, Vla, Cello, Bass, Kybd String Reduction

30/3408L	Full Score
30/3409L	Set of Parts
30/3410L	CD with Printable Parts
30/3411L	Full Score and Parts plus CD with Printable Parts

PRODUCTION NOTES

Some of the cover-art images and graphics from this work are available as free downloads. We hope that you can use them to assist in the making of your bulletins, posters, flyers, website and email announcements, and in any other way that's within your organization and in conjunction with performances of this work.

To access these files, please visit www.lorenz.com/downloads and navigate to the desired folder. PC users should right click and choose "Save Target As…" and Macintosh users should click and hold the link, then choose "Save Target As…" We have provided standard file formats that should be usable in most page layout or word processing software.

Due to the vast number of differences in computer system setups, we are unable to provide technical support for downloadable images/graphics by either phone or email.

PERFORMANCE NOTES FROM THE COMPOSER

Christ's journey to the cross is filled with images that serve as vivid reminders of His sacrificial love for us. These images are the centerpiece of **Come to the Cross and Remember**.

During the cantata's performance, symbols of these images are brought forth to create a tableau. There are two main options for tableau staging:

1) Mount a cross about five feet tall to the left of the choir (stage right). At the center of the cross, place a small nail on which to hang a crown of thorns. Also drill holes on the cross at the traditional position of the hands and feet for the placement of nails.

2) For a simpler option, at center stage place an altar table on which a small "tabletop" cross rests. During the performance, place all symbols in a graceful manner around the tabletop cross.

One or more individuals will bring each symbol forward during the interlude songs, whose tempos are ideal to stepping naturally on the beat. These individuals should dress in a discreet robe or black apparel. They should hold the objects in both hands approximately shoulder high in order to focus attention on the objects. *NOTE: It is very important for this process to be well-prepared during the choir's final rehearsal/s.*

The symbols may be placed in this sequence as follows:

- **The Palms** – Place them at the foot of the cross at the beginning of *2. The Messiah Has Come.* A sturdy vase could hold some branches in front of the cross's center beam, or a small cup or clasp could be mounted on the lower cross for the insertion of branch stems.
  NOTE: For performances on Palm Sunday, you may wish to open the service with a procession of palm branches. In these instances, save a few palms to lay before the cross at the beginning of 2. The Messiah Has Come.
- **The Bread and the Cup** – Place them on a small table at the center of the cross at the beginning of *3. Bring the Cup and the Bread.*
- **Flowers** – Place them in front of the "bread table" at the beginning of *5. Go to Dark Gethsemane.*
- **Thirty Silver Coins** – At the beginning of *6. Bring the Thirty Silver Coins,* carry the coins in a netted bag or small basket and strew or fan them at the foot of the cross or the "bread table." You also may choose to bring a torch and/or a sword and lean them against the cross/table.
- **The Robe and the Crown** – During *8. Bring the Robe and the Crown,* drape the cloth over the crossbeam in a traditional manner; then, hang the crown of thorns on a small nail just above the cross center.
- **The Nails** – At the beginning of *10. O Sacred Hands Now Wounded,* bring three large nails or railroad spikes and place them into holes that have been pre-drilled in the position of hands and feet.
- **The Shroud** – At the beginning of *12. Hold the Shroud in Your Hands,* drape a shroud on the cross.

Because of my experience as a church choir director, I always design my cantatas for performance by choirs both large and small. This worship experience is approximately 35 minutes long and includes narration for one or more speakers, and optional duet and solo. Pages for optional congregational singing are available as a free download. Visit www.lorenz.com and search for 55/1183L. This cantata may be performed with piano accompaniment or Michael Lawrence's captivating full orchestration.

-Pepper Choplin

Prologue

1. Come to the Cross and Remember

Unison with opt. Congregation

Words and Music by
Pepper Choplin

Narrator: *(begin at m. 3)* Today we gather at the cross to bring symbols of Jesus' passion and suffering. As we bring the palm branches and the garden flowers,

the bread and the cup, the betrayer's silver and the angry mob's torch, the crown of thorns and the shroud of the tomb, we will follow Christ's journey to the cross.

☐ indicates CD track number.

© 2017 Lorenz Publishing Company, a division of The Lorenz Corporation. All rights reserved. Printed in U.S.A.
Reproduction of this publication without permission of the publisher is a criminal offense subject to prosecution.
THE CCLI LICENSE DOES NOT GRANT PERMISSION TO PHOTOCOPY THIS MUSIC.

days; all the love Je - sus showed_ as He

walked the fi - nal road. Come re - mem - ber,_ come re -

Narrator: *(begin at m. 18)* Lord, as we begin the journey to the cross, we bring palm branches to remember how

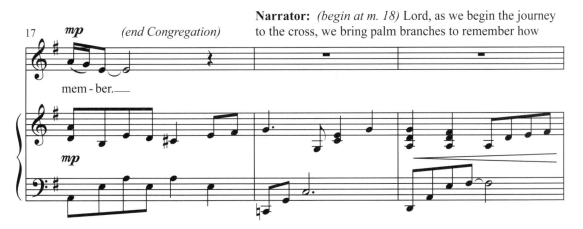

mem - ber._ *(end Congregation)*

the crowds first filled the streets to welcome You with praise. We lift our voices to raise the call, "Hosanna, blessed is He who comes in the name of the Lord."

2. The Messiah Has Come

SATB

Words and Music by
Pepper Choplin

(As music begins, bring palm branches to the cross.)

With sparkling articulation ♩. = ca. 60

*Bring your palm branch-es; there's joy in the street. "Ho-

san-na, ho-san-na," the voic-es re-peat. There is shout-ing and wav-ing to

* Accent the consonants on each downbeat to add extra sparkle throughout.

© 2006 and this edition published in 2017 Lorenz Publishing Company, a division of The Lorenz Corporation.
All rights reserved. Printed in U.S.A.
Reproduction of this publication without permission of the publisher is a criminal offense subject to prosecution.
THE CCLI LICENSE DOES NOT GRANT PERMISSION TO PHOTOCOPY THIS MUSIC.

this bless-ed one, for this is the day the Mes - si - ah has come.

Join the pro - ces - sion and burst in - to song, and

join with the voic - es of heav - en's great throng. There's

prais - ing, cel - e - brat - ing that___ nev - er is done, for

this is the day the Mes - si - ah has come.

cresc.

Look in the fac - es; the__ pain melts a - way, for years__ of pray-ing are

The__ cry - ing and griev - ing for__ an - swered to - day.

now, it is done, for this is the day the Mes - si - ah has

the Lord is here!

head, the Lord is here!

Join the pro - ces - sion and burst in - to song, and join with the voic - es of

heav - en's great throng. There's prais - ing, cel - e - brat - ing that

3. Bring the Cup and the Bread

Unison with opt. Congregation

Words and Music by
Pepper Choplin

(As music begins, bring the cup and the bread to the cross.)

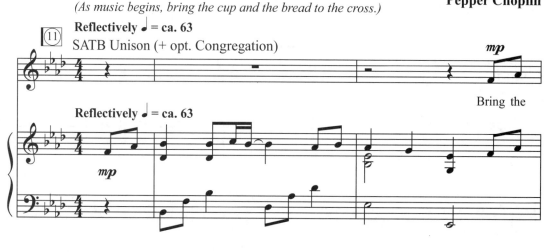

© 2017 Lorenz Publishing Company, a division of The Lorenz Corporation. All rights reserved. Printed in U.S.A.
Reproduction of this publication without permission of the publisher is a criminal offense subject to prosecution.
THE CCLI LICENSE DOES NOT GRANT PERMISSION TO PHOTOCOPY THIS MUSIC.

4. Love Filled the Cup

SATB

Narrator: (*as music begins*) The bread and the cup remind us how You met with Your disciples in the upper room. We reflect on all You said in Your final hours with Your closest friends.

Whenever we eat the bread and drink the cup, we remember how You gave Your life for us.

Come, take the cup,

Come, take the cup; come, take the

for they are poured out and bro - ken for___

bread,

you.

Love filled the

gently

come, take the bread, poured out and

cup and take the bread,

bro - ken for you.

Fa - ther, I am Your Son; now come and make them one,

20

one through love,

so that the world will see their love and u - ni - ty,

and all will know,

21

55/1183&84L-21

The Flowers, Thirty Silver Coins, Torch and Sword

5. Go to Dark Gethsemane

SATB or Unison* with opt. Congregation

Words by **Pepper Choplin**

Arranged by **Pepper Choplin**
Tune: REDHEAD
by **Richard Redhead**, 1853

* If preferred, Unison voices or a Soloist may sing the melody throughout.

© 2017 Lorenz Publishing Company, a division of The Lorenz Corporation. All rights reserved. Printed in U.S.A.
Reproduction of this publication without permission of the publisher is a criminal offense subject to prosecution.
THE CCLI LICENSE DOES NOT GRANT PERMISSION TO PHOTOCOPY THIS MUSIC.

ne ... as we bring the gar - den's

flowers. ... "Take this cup a - way from

Me." ... Hear Him pray that dark - est

hour. "Not My will; I am Your Son.

Let Your ho - ly will be done."

Narrator: *(begin at m. 22; music ends before narration finishes)* Lord, we bring these flowers and remember Your distress as You prayed in the garden of Gethsemane. We recall Your prayer of anguish, "If it be Thy will, take this cup from Me." *(pause)* Lord, though it would mean tremendous suffering, You submitted to the Father's purpose and prayed, "Not My will but Thine be done." *(Continued on next page)*

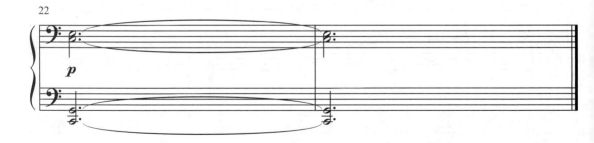

6. Bring the Thirty Silver Coins

Unison with opt. Congregation

Words and Music by
Pepper Choplin

(Narration continues as music begins and coins, torch and/or sword are brought forward.)
We remember that it was also there in the garden that Judas betrayed You and led a mob
with torches and swords to arrest You.

stand

SATB Unison (+ opt. Congregation)

Bring the thir-ty sil-ver coins ___ and re-

mem-ber how ___ Ju - das be-trayed Him for this

© 2017 Lorenz Publishing Company, a division of The Lorenz Corporation. All rights reserved. Printed in U.S.A.
Reproduction of this publication without permission of the publisher is a criminal offense subject to prosecution.
THE CCLI LICENSE DOES NOT GRANT PERMISSION TO PHOTOCOPY THIS MUSIC.

7. Judas

SATB

Words and Music by
Pepper Choplin

© 2017 Lorenz Publishing Company, a division of The Lorenz Corporation. All rights reserved. Printed in U.S.A.
Reproduction of this publication without permission of the publisher is a criminal offense subject to prosecution.
THE CCLI LICENSE DOES NOT GRANT PERMISSION TO PHOTOCOPY THIS MUSIC.

could you come to this? You be - tray Him with your kiss, with your

kiss of treach-er - y, and your kiss will sure-ly lead to His

death!

8. Bring the Robe and the Crown

Unison with opt. Congregation

Words and Music by
Pepper Choplin

(As music begins, bring the robe and the crown to the cross.)

With a sense of gravity ♩ = ca. 63

SATB Unison (+opt. Congregation)

Bring the robe and crown of thorns___ and re-mem-ber___ how they called Je-sus, "King___ of the Jews." But they mocked Him with the name___ and___

© 2017 Lorenz Publishing Company, a division of The Lorenz Corporation. All rights reserved. Printed in U.S.A.
Reproduction of this publication without permission of the publisher is a criminal offense subject to prosecution.
THE CCLI LICENSE DOES NOT GRANT PERMISSION TO PHOTOCOPY THIS MUSIC.

heaped up-on Him shame. We re - mem - ber,____ we re -

(end Congregation)

Narrator: *(begin at m. 13)* Lord, as we bring the purple robe and crown of thorns, we think of all the suffering

mem - ber.____

You endured. We remember the whip on Your back, the fists on Your face, and all the taunts and mockery You suffered. *(pause)* We are reminded of Isaiah's prophecy,

"Surely He has borne our griefs and has carried our sorrows. He was wounded for our transgressions and bruised for our iniquities. The chastisement of our peace was upon

Him, and with His stripes we are healed." *(Isaiah 53:4-5)*   *(end Narration)*

With appreciation to my daugher, Erin

9. Surely He Has Borne Our Griefs

SATB

Words Based on
Isaiah 53:4-5

Words and Music by
Pepper Choplin

Slowly, with passion ♩ = ca. 58

(mp)

SA

mp

Sure-ly___ He has___ borne our griefs, and

mf

He___ has___ car-ried___ all our sor - rows; yet

mf

pressing forward

we have___ thought___ Him___ to be strick - en, struck

pressing forward

© 2017 Lorenz Publishing Company, a division of The Lorenz Corporation. All rights reserved. Printed in U.S.A.
Reproduction of this publication without permission of the publisher is a criminal offense subject to prosecution.
THE CCLI LICENSE DOES NOT GRANT PERMISSION TO PHOTOCOPY THIS MUSIC.

44

The Nails
10. O Sacred Hands, Now Wounded
SATB with opt. Congregation

Words by
Pepper Choplin

Arranged by **Pepper Choplin**
Tune: PASSION CHORALE
by **Hans Leo Hassler**, 1601

(As music begins, bring nails forward and slowly place them in holes on the cross.)

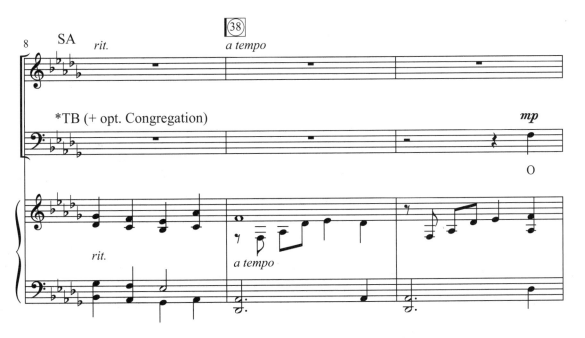

*If congregation sings, unison SATB choir should sing the melody in mm. 10-18.

© 2017 Lorenz Publishing Company, a division of The Lorenz Corporation. All rights reserved. Printed in U.S.A.
Reproduction of this publication without permission of the publisher is a criminal offense subject to prosecution.
THE CCLI LICENSE DOES NOT GRANT PERMISSION TO PHOTOCOPY THIS MUSIC.

sa - cred hands, now wound - ed and nailed up - on— a

the feet that walked on wa - ter are

tree;

pierced by cru - el - ty. How could— love be so

In memory of my friend, David Franklin Jones, forever eighteen

11. You Will Be with Me in Paradise

SATB with opt. Duet and Solo

Words and Music by
Pepper Choplin

Narrator: Lord, when we see the nails, we remember how You were crucified on the cross. Even in the midst of Your great suffering, You prayed for Your tormentors, "Father, forgive them, for they know not what they do." Near the end of Your life, You even showed mercy to a man who was crucified by Your side. We echo his words when he said, "Remember me when You come into Your kingdom." Lord, we carry Your response with us until the end of our days. And when we say goodbye to a loved one, we find comfort when we hear Your words, "You will be with Me in paradise." *(music begins)*

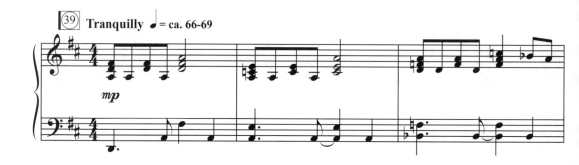

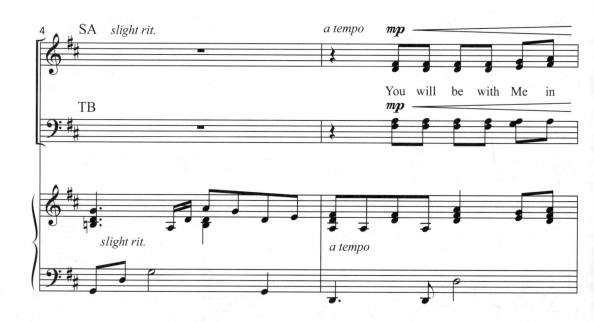

© 2017 Lorenz Publishing Company, a division of The Lorenz Corporation. All rights reserved. Printed in U.S.A.
Reproduction of this publication without permission of the publisher is a criminal offense subject to prosecution.
THE CCLI LICENSE DOES NOT GRANT PERMISSION TO PHOTOCOPY THIS MUSIC.

par - a - dise.   You will be with Me in

par - a - dise.   You will be with Me in

simile

simile

40

par - a - dise.   You will be with Me in

only hope for heav-en. I put my
trust in You— a - lone. Re-mem-ber
me in— par - a-dise.

SA
You will be with Me in par - a-dise.

TB

You will be with Me in par - a - dise.

You will be with Me in par - a - dise.

You will be with Me in par - a - dise.

Solo (or a few women)

When my bod-y is just too wea-ry to live an-oth-er day on this earth. Lord, lift me up in-to Your King-dom and give my soul a sec-ond

43

house _____ are man-y man-sions. I'll pre-

in My Fa-ther's house are man-y man-sions. I'll pre-

pare a place for you. In My Fa-ther's

pare a place for you.

62

12. Hold the Shroud in Your Hands

Unison with opt. Congregation

Words and Music by
Pepper Choplin

Narrator: *(as music begins; bring shroud forward and drape it on the cross.)* At about noon, the sun stopped shining, and darkness came over the whole land until three in the afternoon.

Then the curtain of the temple was torn in two. Jesus called out with a loud voice, "Father, into Your hands I commit My spirit." When He had said this, He breathed His last.

SATB Unison (+ opt. Congregation)

(end Narration)

Hold the shroud in your hands— and re- mem - ber how His bod - y was wrapped in - to the

© 2017 Lorenz Publishing Company, a division of The Lorenz Corporation. All rights reserved. Printed in U.S.A.
Reproduction of this publication without permission of the publisher is a criminal offense subject to prosecution.
THE CCLI LICENSE DOES NOT GRANT PERMISSION TO PHOTOCOPY THIS MUSIC.

LT

cloth. In the grave's dark-ened room,— they—

sealed Him in a tomb. We re-mem-ber,— we re-

Narrator: *(begin at m. 16)*
Lord, we remember how they quietly lowered Your lifeless body from the cross and wrapped it in a shroud. Then, as

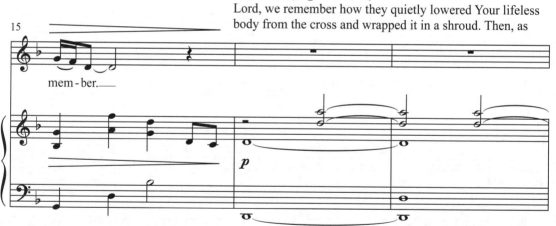

mem-ber.—

night was falling, they laid Your body in the grave and sealed it in the tomb.

(end Narration)

13. Waitin' for the Mornin'

SATB with opt. Descant

Words and Music by
Pepper Choplin

© 2014 and this edition published in 2017 Lorenz Publishing Company, a division of The Lorenz Corporation.
All rights reserved. Printed in U.S.A.
Reproduction of this publication without permission of the publisher is a criminal offense subject to prosecution.
THE CCLI LICENSE DOES NOT GRANT PERMISSION TO PHOTOCOPY THIS MUSIC.

55/1183&84L-65

LT

ag - o - ny, I'm wait-in' for the morn - in'

when the sun is gon-na rise, gon-na rise

up! I'm wait-in' and though the shad-ows of

cresc.

f

pain and death___ try to shroud my soul___ with

hope - less - ness, I'm wait - in' for the morn - in'

when the sun is gon - na rise.___

up! And when— the dark - ness tries to o - ver - come, it won't

last for - ev - er and will soon— be done, so I'm

wait - in' for the morn - in' when the sun is gon - na

Finale
14. Every Knee Shall Bow
SATB

Words Based on
Philippians 2:6-11

Words and Music by
Pepper Choplin

Narrator: Through Christ, we can have hope, even in the darkest of times. And though the night of death may overtake us, a new morning will surely come, and the sun will surely rise. *(pause as music begins)*

(Narration resumes with strength at m.4)
Christ humbled Himself by becoming obedient unto death, even death on a cross. Therefore God also

has highly exalted Him, and has given Him a name which is above every name: that at the name of Jesus

every knee should bow, of things in heaven, and things in earth, and things under the earth; and that

every tongue should confess that Jesus Christ is Lord, to the glory of God the Father. *(end Narration)*

© 2017 Lorenz Publishing Company, a division of The Lorenz Corporation. All rights reserved. Printed in U.S.A.
Reproduction of this publication without permission of the publisher is a criminal offense subject to prosecution.
THE CCLI LICENSE DOES NOT GRANT PERMISSION TO PHOTOCOPY THIS MUSIC.

name of Je - sus, ev - 'ry tongue con - fess that the
name of Je - sus is high a - bove all names. Let
ev - 'ry voice pro - claim,___ "Christ is Lord."

name of Je - sus, ev - 'ry tongue con - fess that the

name of Je - sus is high a - bove all names. Let

[63]

ev - 'ry voice pro - claim,___ "Christ is Lord. He is